You Walk Pretty

LeAnne Nelson Dahl

LeAnne N Dahl

763-289-4721

PublishAmerica
Baltimore

© 2005 by LeAnne Nelson Dahl.
All rights reserved. No part of this book may be reproduced, stored in a retrieval system or transmitted in any form or by any means without the prior written permission of the publishers, except by a reviewer who may quote brief passages in a review to be printed in a newspaper, magazine or journal.

First printing

ISBN: 1-4137-8384-8
PUBLISHED BY PUBLISHAMERICA, LLLP
www.publishamerica.com
Baltimore

Printed in the United States of America

In loving memory of my parents, Al and Mae Nelson, who taught me to never give up.

The author wishes to express her sincere appreciation to Rianne Leaf for her invaluable help in editing and preparing this book for publication. Gratitude also goes to Debbie Meile for her assistance whenever the author needed to look her best.

-LND

Darla lived a few doors away.
This five-year-old
Walked by one day.

She stopped to watch me
As I took a few faltering steps
across the lawn.
She didn't know I had CP.

"You walk pretty," I heard her say.
"Thank you," I replied.
And she skipped away.

© LeAnne Nelson Dahl
March 2005

Foreword

Yes, LeAnne does walk pretty…in spirit, in determination, in kindness, and in support and encouragement to other people wherever she is.

As readers will find through her poems, LeAnne responded well to life despite periods of concern about her disability and frustration at not being able to do everything she wanted to do, as well as some sad, lonely, and trying times. Readers will be moved by her joy, humor, compassion, strength, and deep faith that have really defined who she is.

Those of us who have known LeAnne for decades are so pleased she has captured the essence of herself and her life in these poems.

Thank you, LeAnne, for being so willing to share your life with any and all who pick up this little book. You have "walked pretty"!

-Rianne Leaf

Introduction

Memories can be wonderful ~
    Full of warmth, humor, and tender moments.
    Filled with both happiness and sadness.
    That's what my first sixty-five years have been made up of…
        Plus so much more.
    This book is dedicated to all the special people
        Who surround me now ~ and
            All those who have traveled on to a far better place
                called Heaven.

Some may find this hard to believe,
But my first memories are from the time I was two or younger.
        It's a well known fact that elephants have long
            memories.
        Well, I think I have them beat.

Oh, speaking of animals and before I get into the more personal recollections, let me tell you what my favorite animals are and why.
        It isn't elephants.

        I love birds because they can fly free.
        (That is, with the exception of my wonderful
            parakeet, Humphrey.
        Humphrey keeps me company from his cage
            beside my computer.
        He loves when I'm typing and listening to the TV.
        But he becomes jealous and tries to compete
            with me
        when I'm on the phone.)

Dogs are very close to my heart.
They understand emotions and love unconditionally.

Chimpanzees drive me into hysterics with their antics.
They remind me that sometimes, as human beings, we all do idiotic things ~ causing others to laugh or become angry.

I'm sure that within the past six and a half decades,
I have done both.

Interspersed among my poems are reflections that may give more details.
These poems were written during the summer of 2003.
I wrote them out of a need to make some sense out of life.
I needed to close a few chapters and begin looking ahead…
    To my "golden years."

You Walk Pretty

The Growing Up Years

When I was small
I thought I had it all.
Mom, Dad, and me.
Just us three.
    But then the news came,
    with no one to blame.
    The diagnosis was C.P.
My Dad did say
exercise would pay.
So Mom taught me to walk,
despite my balk.
    First I walked with a harness,
    then along a rope.
        With each step
          she prayed I would learn to cope
          with what I needed to accept in time,
          and hoping it was peace I'd find.
Both parents encouraged me to try
to do my best, even if I'd cry.

I wouldn't have reached any goals
without their good hearts and souls.
    Dad wanted me to attend school,
    but Mom didn't think that was so cool.
        She wouldn't even discuss it with Dad
        because she felt so bad.
    In fact, each one worked with me in different ways.
    Dad kept my mind stimulated,
    while Mom exercised me.

My parents and I were very close.
Although Dad didn't earn a lot,
I always felt we were rich.

Mom and Dad never let me feel that
I was in their way
or making their life harder
because of my C.P.

Reflections on My Parents

Of course, everyone believes they have the best parents.
BUT I KNOW I had the best parents for me. Al and Mae (Hakko) Nelson were given a tough task to do in raising a daughter born with cerebral palsy.

My parents, having never experienced parenthood before, didn't know what to expect. Yet, they began searching for answers when I didn't start sitting up and doing the normal activities babies do. When the first doctor couldn't answer their questions, they looked for other doctors until they found an osteopath
    who diagnosed me as having C.P.

I vividly remember Mom giving me warm baths each morning and then exercising my legs. She walked me around the living room while hanging on to my harness so I wouldn't fall. The minute she let go, down I'd fall.

You may not believe this, but I remember my first day of school ~ my first day of kindergarten. I came home on that big yellow bus all by myself.
For Mom, this was a day she did not look forward to or want to happen. Every time Dad talked about my going to school,
    she'd change the subject.

I'll always be thankful that Dad insisted on my having a good education, even though I did not attend college. Mom and Dad both worked very hard with me, especially through high school.
Dad urged me to keep learning and use my time wisely because he said I would have to work with my mental abilities rather than my physical abilities. He was right!

The three of us were always a very close family unit. My parents took me with them wherever they went. Before I walked, they carried me. I never felt embarrassed or self-conscious ~ until the age of eleven.

The Learning Years

I loved to learn!
School was fun at every turn ~
especially my high school years.
My memories are so dear.

    Mom wrote my math for me.
    The teacher graded Mom ~ then me.
    She always received a higher grade
    Than what I made.

Then graduation time was near,
I did shed many a tear.
I hated to leave school
Because I didn't know what else to do.

    Mom and Dad were proud as could be!
    All three of us graduated, you see.
    We needed to rest.
    That was for the best.

The Tough Years

School was so much a part of me.
Now how could I be
Without it?
All I did was sit.

It was obvious college wasn't for me.
My life seemed so empty ~
There were no plans in sight,
My future didn't look bright.

Dad's health had turned bad,
Which made Mom and me sad.
Dad made a big choice.
We really didn't have a voice.

Moving was his decision.
That's when Dad and I had a collision.
I plainly did not want to go
And I hit an all time low.

I often wonder where I would be if I had gone to college.
For years, I berated myself for not going.
Yet, as maturity set in,
I realized it was a blessing.

People would say, "It's never too late, you can still go."
Others asked, "What college did you attend?"

I believed then, as I do now,
That a higher education would not have helped me
Become employed.
It probably would have frustrated me more.

My Faith

I may not speak of it often or at all,
Yet it's part of my entire soul.
    It's there for me when I fall,
    Knowing I'll never be whole.

I learned two religions from Mom and Dad,
One was a Christian, the other was a Jew.
    Two more loving teachers I never had.
    It took a while before I knew…

What faith I would follow.
How could I hurt either one?
    I did not want to appear shallow
    By saying one lost, the other won.

Both religions teach what is right,
This was not my fear,
    Of that I never lost sight.
    Now I see that it was clear.

I chose to be a Christian.
I felt it was right for me.
    Dad backed my decision.
    Once more, he had set me free.

Although Mom was glad,
She didn't show any emotion.
    She had too much love for Dad.
    Mom was a very private person.

The Move

We moved from Chicago to St. Paul.
It was a very long haul.
I hated leaving my friends.
    I felt as though my life was at the end.

I didn't know what would happen to me.
There was no future I could see.
Dad wanted me to work with him.
    That sounded pretty grim.

During the summer of 1959
I met a young man through friends.
He was attending a camp for the disabled in Indiana.
    I persuaded my parents to let me go.

By the time I returned from camp
    David and I thought we were in love.

Of course my parents were upset
Because there was no way this could work.
David's C.P. was more severe than mine ~
    One more reason our move was so crucial.

The day of the move I locked myself in the bathroom.
    Life would never be the same.

Bouts with Depression

When I was eight, it began.
I don't know how or why.
Since then, it occurred again.
I never know how or why.
    This ugly thing is called depression.
    It hits me when I least expect it.
    Sometimes it causes regression ~
    It feels like I'm in a pit.
I hoped it would go away.
But it still comes and goes
Even if I pray.
Why? God only knows.

A Job

I wanted a job of my own
Now that I was grown.
But having a disability,
Who would believe I had any ability?

My parents had faith in me.
They said, "You'll see."
Of course, I didn't believe them.
My question was, "When?"

My Dad's Nature

My Dad was a serious man who didn't put up with any nonsense.
He raised me to use my brains instead of my limbs.

He was well aware of what lay ahead of me.
His biggest concern was that I would be left alone
When he and mother were gone.

He was a self-educated man who only finished eighth grade,
But insisted that I get as much education as possible.

He was a stern father with a soft heart.
As my cousin said once, "His spankings for you are only like love taps."
And they were.

I always knew that he loved me.
He didn't want me to experience the dark side of life.
His philosophy was, "Either I would love him or hate him for what
He taught me." And of course I loved him.

I wished with all my heart that I could have done things for and with Dad.
He was a very good man.

At the time of his death I was like a child.
Yet, I believe that he would be proud of me today.

My Dear Dad

You were here a short time.
    You were so loving and kind.
    You taught me so much.
    You and Mom never left me behind.

You were here a short time
    But I remember how you instilled
    In me to keep trying
    And never lose my will.

You were here a short time.
    You taught me to respect everyone,
    No matter who
    Or where they came from.

You were here a short time.
    You accepted my disability,
    And you instructed me
    To use my creativity.

You were here a short time.
    You encouraged me
    To become involved with others
    In order to set myself free.

You were here a short time.
    You said, "Look to God for guidance.
    He'll keep you in His loving care,
    So listen as He speaks in silence."

You were here a short time.
    You never saw the woman I grew to be.
    I've tried to live up to your values.
    I hope in some way you CAN see.

I haven't done all I could do,
   But in some small way
   I hope I have made you
   PROUD this Father's Day.

The Climb Up

Dad planned ahead.
    When he was dead
    The house turned out to be
    What kept us debt-free.

The third floor we rented out
    To men who were stout.
    They worked for the State.
    As tenants, they were first rate.

Mom cared for the house and lawn.
    She always rose about dawn.
    This kept her from thinking about Dad
    All the time, and feeling so bad.

It became hard for her to read.
    I helped fill her every need
    By reading everything to her.
    Mom counted on me to be there.

Whereas she did the same for me
    By helping me with things
    I couldn't do ~
    That turned out to be quite a few.

Mom and I were always close,
    Of that I can boast.
    We were like two peas in a pod
    Under the watch of God.

A Difficulty

It's very difficult to find the words to write about my aunt. She resented me because she thought that I got all the attention she wanted.

After going through years of therapy, I realize how much I blamed myself and how guilt ridden I have felt.

Now I see and feel that the past can no longer hurt or taunt me.

My Aunt, the Other Side

Why did I allow her to hurt me?
    She claimed I was her favorite at first ~
    I, her niece.
    Years later my bubble burst.
Why did I allow her to hurt me?
    She did it in such a way
    That everyone thought she treated me well.
    They never heard what she could say.
Why did I allow her to hurt me?
    Did I feel ashamed
    Or wrong?
    I felt I was the one to be blamed.

Why did I allow her to hurt me?
    I married to get out of her way.
    At the time it seemed right ~
    And did it make her day!
Why did I allow her to hurt me?
    I was afraid of my aunt.
    She could be nice one minute,
    Then turn to rave and rant.
Why did I allow her to hurt me?
    She pushed and shoved.
    She didn't care.
    I tried to handle her, gloved.

Why did I allow her to hurt me?
    She wanted to be catered to.
    She wanted pity, but more than that,
    She enjoyed telling others what to do.
Why did I allow her to hurt me?
    She never believed anything I said.
    She insinuated I lied,
    Then believed others instead.

Why did I allow her to hurt me?
   I really do not know.
   Perhaps I never will.
   Could it be to let me grow?

Anger

Do I have anger?
    Of course I do.
    It's not easy to conquer.

Angry at whom?
    Mostly at myself,
    But what can I do?

I wanted to help Mother more.
    I didn't like seeing her struggle.
    I couldn't even take her to the store.

My lack of coordination
    In my hands and legs
    Is a big frustration.

I find it hard to cope
    When there are things to be done.
    I feel as though I am at the end of my rope.

Yet, it's not God I'm angry at
    Once I calm down and listen.
    I just need His loving pat.

Late Bloomer

I needed to spread my wings,
But where would I find some things
To keep me busy and productive?
Where can I give?

I was afraid to explore.
Yet I had to open the door
To find what was out there ~
And where.

Self Image

I never liked looking in the mirror.
I've always felt self-conscious.
I could feel people staring at me ~
Cerebral palsy makes them curious.

    The effects of C.P.
    Are not easy to see.
    Let's face it,
    Why would anyone want to be me?

But God has blessed me
With many friends
Who see beyond my shell.

        I needed to be strong,
        Not weak.
        I had to learn to fight
        My battle of being meek.

This was and will be ongoing
Day in and day out.
Some days I'm happy,
Other days I pout.

My Angels

God sent special people to me
To guide and allow me to see
There were things I could do
To help others, too.

    The first was a neat gal.
    She became a pal.
    She taught me typing and much more.
    Esther was never a bore.

        Then came Janice and Bob.
        Together we laugh and we sob.
        Lifelong friends are hard to find,
        But they are two of a kind.

Christian League was my introduction
To begin writing for mass production.
Bob and Janice saw to that.
For me, they went to bat.

    Bob asked me to speak
    One evening. I grew weak,
    So I took a little pill ~
    Then my speech fit the bill.

        He's never let me forget
        That was the start of it ~
        My speaking in front of others ~
        To the surprise of Mother.

Sometimes

What I could not see
Were the "some times"
That came and went
Between the "sad times"
If this or that took place.

That's what I thought,
But I couldn't live that way.
I needed to go after whatever I sought.

My Cerebral Palsy

It was there from the start.
It will never depart.
For short, it's called C.P.
What does it mean to me?
    Although I've had a lifelong disability since birth,
    I've never been angry at God ~
    Nor have I blamed anyone.
    It's just something that is.
    While I've lived without physical pain,
    My heart and soul have felt the strain.
    I've felt inferior to all.
    Inside, I did bawl.
There are worse things in this world to deal with than C.P.
I see this now at the age of sixty-four
with all of life's difficult problems behind me.
    As a child I was happy,
    But my teens were crappy.
    The older I grew,
    I knew I had to make do.

While most people view this time in their life
As being on their downward slope,
I see this as a time to reflect on one's self
And establish a peace with one's self.
    They say life can be rough ~
    One must learn to be tough.
    That just wasn't in my character.
    Did it imply I must become an actor?
Where once I couldn't wait until
A certain time came or a certain event occurred,
Now I no longer eagerly await these things,
For nothing seems that important anymore.
    I tried to hide the things I couldn't do,
    Hoping no one really knew

How hard tasks were for me.
　　　I didn't want any pity.
No longer is my disability a threat to me.
I can't be something I'm not.
I have accepted my lot.
　　　It took many trials and mistakes
　　　Before I made the break
　　　With my past.

I'm enjoying my life maybe for the first time.
I don't have to cater to anyone.
I've started fresh at last.

It Hurts Me

Do you know how it feels
To have someone pity you?
For some, it may not be a big deal,
But it hurts me, making me feel blue.

I cannot stand someone who
Always seems to mean well,
Yet flaunts that they're better off than you,
Trying to be your pal.

Somehow I must find a way
To rise above the crushing blow
And learn how to say
"Look beyond my shell and see my soul!"

Frightened Again

Did I act too friendly?
   I didn't mean to.
   I'm feeling badly.

Did I give the wrong impression?
   I've become leery
   Of men with obsessions.

The experience I had last year
Taught me to be less trusting.
I need to make myself clear ~
I have to put an end
To this man's bad conduct,
But it's a matter of how and when.

Mom's Illness

It began with a shot for flu.
This was Mom's first one ever.
Three months later we knew
Her life had changed forever.

    For nine weeks she endured
    The hospital stay,
    But the medical team said she couldn't be cured.
    There just was no way.

At last a diagnosis was made:
Guillian Barre or French Polio, it's named.
Poor Mom, in bed she laid.
It was the flu shot we blamed.

    She began physical therapy
    And occupational therapy, too.
    Every little progress made me happy.
    What next? We didn't have a clue.

Mom's Outcome

Mom never returned home again.
She needed more therapy and care.
It was hard to comprehend
Why she had so much to bear.

We moved Mom to a nursing home
Three miles away
So she wouldn't feel that alone.
Little did we know it's where she'd stay.

For a while therapy went well.
Mom kept improving every day,
But her house we had to sell
She decided, and had her say.

Mom never made a full recovery.
Her mind remained alert until the end,
But a wheelchair was her mobility.
I had her, although she didn't mend.

Six and a half years went by.
We shared many precious days.
I wasn't ready for her to die,
But the Lord took her anyway.

My Dear Mother

Mother, you will never know
How much I miss you ~
    Your quiet strength,
    Your strong faith too.

Mother, you will never know
The wisdom you imparted
    Throughout my life,
    Teaching me to be good-hearted.

Mother, you will never know
How much I appreciate
    The time you spent encouraging me
    To walk with a steady gait.

Mother, you will never know
The strength you gave me
    Through your quiet voice
    That set me free.

Mother, you will never know
How I've become strong
    In so many ways
    Since you've been gone.

Yet, I think you do know
From where you are at rest.
    You've seen all my trials
    And it's worked for the best.
    My biggest regret of all
    Is knowing the worry I caused you
    Over the many struggles.
    I made you blue.

Life is brighter now. I'm finally happy once more.
For me God opened a brand new door.
    I've reached the top of that hill
    You, Dad, and I were climbing.
    The path was rough and steep.
    Now church bells are chiming.

Mother dear, rest in peace.
Your work on earth is truly done.
    No longer fear for me ~
    Your race is won.

Sixteen Years

Sixteen years is a long time
To be miserable secretly.
    I hid it from everyone.
    This was hard on me.

Sixteen years is a long time
To let others believe
    Our marriage was so great,
    When they were being deceived.

Sixteen years is a long time
To feel as though you owe
    Something to your spouse
    For rescue from a foe.

Sixteen years is a long time
To always try to please your spouse,
    Yet never quite able to do
    Anything right in the house.

Sixteen years is a long time
To live with both our disabilities,
    And trying to cope
    With all the responsibilities.

The Stroke

Another disability appeared
When a stroke hit my spouse in 1998.
It's a miracle he was spared,
But the damage was great.

His right side was attacked:
It was difficult for him to talk.
He fought hard to get back:
With a cane he had to walk.

Life became more of a struggle.
I did all I could for him,
But it wasn't quite enough ~
Our spirits grew grim.

We needed more help
So we hired Kim.
She was an answer to prayer.
Life seemed no longer dim.

Over the Next Two Years

Over the next two years
I tried harder than ever
To make life happier,
But I wasn't very clever.

    I got a recommendation
    For a person to write out bills.
    Soon he became our POA,
    But he turned out to be a bad deal.

        I became nervous and depressed.
        Our marriage was nearing the end.
        I knew it was coming,
        But I didn't know how or when.

I called our doctor finally.
We went for an office call.
He had me in one room
And my spouse down the hall.

    The doctor hardly understood my speech.
    He knew he had to do something fast.
    It was his decision
    That began my break with the past.

The Married Years~Over

WHY is divorce so hard?
   Even if it was right for me,
   It still hurts
   To say that I'm free.

WHY is divorce so hard?
   Why was I never right
   According to him?
   Yet, he wanted me in his sight.

WHY is divorce so hard?
   Why couldn't I be happy
   When he was around?
   Why was he so crabby?

WHY is divorce so hard?
   Like all couples
   We thought we'd never part.
   The marriage was wrong from the start.

WHY is divorce so hard?
   I wish I knew.
   But it's time to make a new start ~
   It's long overdue.

Another Move

Thank God for friends
Who can respond in a day.
Sabine drove me around.
I found a place to stay.

    One more day passed.
    I made arrangements to relocate.
    Again dear friends helped.
    October twenty-third was the date.

        I had never lived alone.
        It was a little scary
        And exciting at the same time.
        The apartment was nice and airy.

            Kim was my salvation ~
            She kept working for me.
            I still had much to face ~
            Divorce was the key.

Beginning a New Life

It was hard at first
To believe I was on my own.
This day took a long time coming.

How could I have known
The twists and turns
My life was taking?

Now I would go another way,
Hoping my heart would stop aching.
Kim suggested a Holiday Party.

Many friends came to see
My new home and me.
I was as happy as could be.

Another Transition

Life changes from day to day.
We never know what to expect
Or what takes place
That will have a profound effect.

I wanted nothing more
Than to live on my own,
But God closed that door.
He didn't want me living alone.

Instead God brought me
To another kind of home
Where others reside,
Where no one is alone.

Thus my transition began.
It didn't take long
Before I knew it ~
I felt like I belonged.

The Seasons of My Life

The seasons of my life
Have been very interesting.
Not one has been dull.
Yet I'm not prepared for resting.

   Springtime was my best,
   My work made life worth living.
   There was plenty to do.
   I felt good about giving.

      The Summer was long and hard.
      While I hoped for the easiest,
      Mom and my spouse were my worry.
      It was not my time to rest.

         Autumn is the sweetest time of all
         When life has come together for me.
         I'm enjoying this season ~
         For the first time I feel free.

            Whenever my Winter comes
            I will not mind.
            I thank the good Lord
            And all who have been so kind.

When I Was Five

The spring I turned five
The boys noticed me
As I played in the yard,
Busy as a bee.

They called to me, but
I could hardly stand on my own.
These teenage boys were quite polite,
They didn't laugh or groan.

They saw my disability,
Cerebral palsy was its name.
I smiled at them,
Too young to feel shame.

These boys returned my smile.
For them and for me
It was the start of a friendship
That brought much glee.

The following Valentine's Day
There was a red heart-shaped box for me
Outside our front door with a card attached
With the boys' names—all three.

Thus began my love of chocolate and boys.
I thought both were sweet,
But years later I discovered
Neither are always so sweet.

The Special Men in My Life

I have been fortunate throughout the years
To have unique friendships with a few gentlemen.
Each one expanded my horizons
And encouraged me to believe in myself again.

I will always cherish these relationships,
Some of which were bittersweet.
I grew as a person from each one;
Therefore, I'm glad we did meet.

Now I'm at a place in life
Where I can sit back,
Relax and enjoy ~
For there's nothing I lack.

Past, Present, and Future

I've spent too much time living with the past.
It's time to live for the moment.
The memories of old will last ~
I cannot lament.

I can't do anything about yesterday,
It's today that matters.
If I had my way
All the bad would shatter.
    The future will appear
    Before I know it.
    No, it isn't clear
    From where I sit.
        I'm no longer apprehensive ~
        What shall be, shall be.
        I know the Lord will give
        His strength to me.

I never envisioned myself grown ~
My C.P. overshadowed everything.
Whatever I dreamt seemed blown.
I couldn't imagine having wings.

        As my teens grew closer
        My self-esteem fell lower.
        I was fearful of future years.
        I anticipated many tears.
    Who would be there for me?
    Would I ever feel free?
    Where would I live?
    What did I have to give?
I felt inferior and low.
How could I be
Without Mom and Dad?
I would always be alone and sad.

I didn't think about or see
What eventually came to be.

At Last

Is this really it, God?
Am I really where you want me?
If it is, I'm thankful
And happy.

Everything fits together
Like a glove:
Good health, food, shelter,
Respect and plenty of love.

There are no more put-downs
Or screaming.
I no longer fear
My future living.

So, from here on
I'll accept what comes my way,
Feeling the Lord's guidance
Each and every day.

Family

During my early years I felt loved
By uncles, aunts, and cousins.
They were all dears.

    There were family get-togethers
    For holidays and birthdays.
    We were in touch with each other.

    Then, as often happens,
    Families drift apart ~
    The closeness dampens.

        Now we are the older ones
        (It doesn't seem possible)
        With daughters and sons.

I married late in life.
After nineteen years it ended.
There was much strife.

    Somehow I knew
    It would turn out like this.
    Love isn't always true.

    I do not know what the family thinks.
    They thought we were a neat pair.
    They didn't see all the kinks.

        I miss not having family around.
        Without friends where would I be?
        They hold me up when I'm down.

Different Kinds of Love

What is LOVE?
And where does it come from?
I believe it comes from God above.

LOVE fits into stages:
    First it starts between parent and child,
    Which takes up many pages.

    Then comes LOVE for siblings ~
    It's not always sweet,
    There can be much quibbling.

LOVE for self is vital,
It implies self respect
Instead of self denial.

    We LOVE our friends
    And they LOVE us
    Until life's end.

If we are lucky to find
That one special person
Who is LOVING and kind,
    We can count our blessings,
    Understanding that God is all-wise,
    Comforting and LOVING.

Humphrey

Humphrey came to me
From Kim, John, and Joe.

He's more than a parakeet ~
He keeps me from being low.

Humphrey earns his keep
By talking in his own way.

He chirps and makes a peep,
Then looks at me as if to say,

> "I'll keep you company
> If you take care of me."

So this little blue bird
Has my heart to keep.

There's Something to Be Said for Aging

I used to try with all my might,
But I could never quite
Succeed at all I wanted to do.
Perhaps I tried to compete, too.

Now that I've relaxed a bit,
I can let my wit
Come out, appearing to all,
While I have a ball.

So aging isn't all that bad.
It doesn't make me sad.
In fact, it gives me an excuse
To feel free and loose.

Laughter

Many funny things happened over the years
Having to do with my disability,
Causing laughter until there were tears.

When I worked as a lobbyist, I met many people.
Abby was an advocate for MN Association for Retarded Citizens,
As well as their lobbyist. We soon became friends.
    Abby and I made an agreement ~
    She would pick me up at home every morning
    And I let her use my parking permit.

I took this friend to a restaurant
For her birthday.
I was very nonchalant.
    The waitress showed us our table
    In the middle of the room.
    She noticed my feet weren't stable.

We both ordered a glass of wine
To relax and unwind
Before we dined.

When our order was being placed,
The waitress treated me
As if I were a mental case.
    She asked my friend if I had made a menu choice.
    My friend said, "Ask her.
    She has her own voice."

At the end of the meal, my friend received the bill.
She turned and said, "Dr. Nelson will pay this."
The poor waitress turned green at the gills.

Wanting to carry on this charade,
I walked over to the cash register
And wrote the check with aid.
    I nearly told the young woman behind
    The counter that I was to perform surgery later.
    I did enjoy that glass of wine.

Vacationing

Leaving home for a short while
Can be fun and relaxing.
It should fit one's style.

But with aging and a disability,
Staying home is better.

Problems with mobility
Make it difficult on everyone.

I am not willing to go again.
My traveling days are done.

Reconnecting

Seeing family once more
Brought so many memories back,
Reaching my heart's core.

They embraced me with open arms.
It felt so great
To again enjoy their charms.

When we said our goodbyes,
I couldn't help but think,
"Was this our last before one of us dies?"

Tears filled my eyes
That no one saw
As I let out a big sigh.

Sixty-Four

Why did it take so long
    To find my place?
To feel like I belong
    To the human race?

With so much behind me
    I still have plenty to do.
I'm as busy as a bee,
    And happier, too.

There will always be pain,
    That's a sure thing ~
Without it there's no gain,
    And that's worth everything.

Happiness

If you could look into my heart today,
I know what it would say:
    "Why did it take you until now
    To find out how?"

Happiness doesn't grow on trees,
Nor does it come from bees.
    It has to be created within
    The heart, without a loud din.

Happiness is like chocolate:
It melts when it's hot.
    But if it cools,
    It leaves you.

Music is a Part of Me

Ever since I can recall
Music has been very special to me ~
It puts me in a lull.

If I listen to lively tunes,
My energy is high
And my heart zooms.

I love classical music to write by.
It brings out my soul ~
Sometimes it makes me cry.

A Relaxed Life

Some people might feel this is the end.
I see assisted living as a fresh start.
It may be hard for others to depend
On a staff at first to do their part.

For myself, I feel blessed.
I know I can't live alone,
And that had to be addressed.
I don't feel I need to be on my own.

It's like a weight is gone ~
I smile and laugh more,
I'm dancing to a new song,
To my friends I'm no longer a bore.

If everyone learned to relax,
Enjoy their surroundings
And forget the past,
There would be joy abounding.

What I Would Do

If I did not have cerebral palsy
There is so much I would do ~
    I would use my time wisely
    And help others, too.

If I did not have cerebral palsy
I would have taught young ones
    To develop their potential to the highest degree.
    They'd use their intellect instead of guns.

If I did not have cerebral palsy
I would drive people around
    To wherever they wanted to go and see,
    So they wouldn't become housebound.

If I did not have cerebral palsy
I'd work in a homeless shelter,
    Hoping to be happy and cheery,
    Trying to wipe out some despair.

However, I do have cerebral palsy.
I'm thankful for what I can do and give.
    Perhaps things don't come easy for me,
    But I will give all I can as long as I live.

It Is Time

It is time to take one last look around
The corners of my mind
To see what's hidden there
That I can tie up and bind.

It is time to extinguish any smoldering
That might linger
Among the rubble
So it won't flicker.

It is time to say goodbye to the past
And greet the present and the future
With enthusiasm,
Knowing it will last.

2004

God, I don't know what You have in store
For me in 2004,
But wherever You lead me
I will be ready to see.

I am no longer full of fear
For You are right here.
You have led me to my life's place ~
All I seek is your grace.

My Faith Today

I have always believed in God.
He has been close to me throughout my life.
There were times of doubt for me,
Especially during hours of strife.

I didn't always understand the Trinity,
And I'm not sure I will ever comprehend
The full beauty of it,
But I know my belief will never end.

I see Jesus all around me ~
He's in the people where I reside,
He's in the staff that care for me.
My faith in Him shall always abide.

I've Been a Lot

Since my birth in 1939
    A lot of changes have taken place.
    C.P. is not so unknown,
    Yet it's still an incurable case.

Since my birth in 1939
    Strides have been made to rid us of
    Intolerance of others,
    Yet we're still lacking brotherly love.

Since my birth in 1939
    Science has developed techniques
    And inventions to make life easier.
    There's something new every few weeks.

Since my birth in 1939
    We believe we're sophisticated.
    But I wonder what God thinks of all this?
    How would we be graded?

To Adults with Disabilities

Living with cerebral palsy is challenging
    But not defeating.
    It may be difficult
    And at times exhausting.

Living with cerebral palsy can be embarrassing.
    The feeling is hard to describe.
    How can one explain that the exterior
    Doesn't resemble the inside?

Living with cerebral palsy day in and day out
    Can be tedious and frustrating.
    Yet giving up is not in our vocabulary,
    It just means more creating.

Living with cerebral palsy involves fighting ~
    Fighting to convince others
    That our feelings are the same as theirs.
    All we need is to be like their sisters and brothers.

Living with cerebral palsy is being realistic
    About the things we can and cannot do,
    Making wise choices about our lives
    Instead of wishing for the moon.

Living with cerebral palsy is not wanting pity
    From family, friends, or strangers.
    We must learn to be strong inside,
    Showing love rather than anger.

To All Parents of Children and Youth with Disabilities

*This comes to you with understanding, appreciation,
But most of all with love.*

I know what patience it takes
To nurture a child with a disability,
To watch with your heart in your throat
Each time he or she falls, knowing it's a reality.

I know what time it takes
To go to doctor and therapy appointments,
To drive, find a close parking space,
Then hurry to find the right departments.

I know how your heart must break
When someone hurts or laughs at your child.
It never really heals,
But you must stay calm and mild.

I know how often you must cry inside
When your daughter is old enough to date,
But no one will ask her,
So you can't watch her go through your gate.

I know all this because I watched my own mother
As she hid her deepest feelings from me.
I longed to tell her she need not worry,
"Someday I will be fine! You'll see."

I know that "Someday" came for my mother,
And it will come for you too.
I'm now in assisted living ~
Her prayer came true.

I know I will be safe and sound
From now on.
It took years, that's for sure,
But all fears are gone.

I know about the love and understanding
Of our parents who encourage
Us to do our best
Until the end of our age

I know we can show our appreciation
By taking responsibility
As much as possible,
Showing our true ability.

Printed in the United States
35891LVS00006B/469-600